The Fall of Apartheid
in South Africa

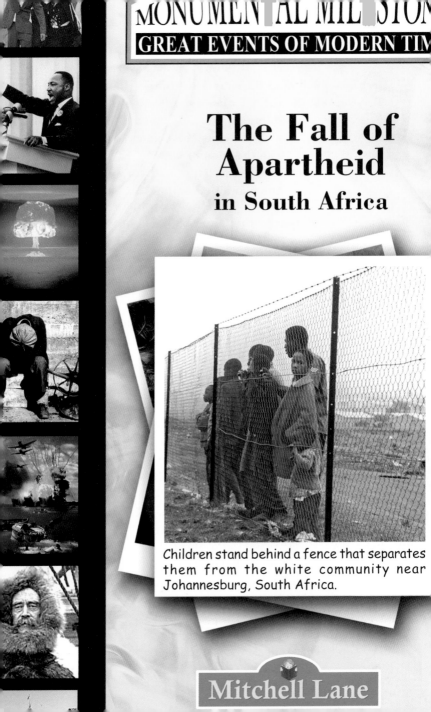

Children stand behind a fence that separates them from the white community near Johannesburg, South Africa.

Mitchell Lane

Titles in the Series

MONUMENTAL MILESTONES
GREAT EVENTS OF MODERN TIMES

The Fall of
Apartheid
in South Africa

Even public benches were not shared.

Melissa Koosmann

PUBLISHERS

Copyright © 2010 by Mitchell Lane Publishers, Inc. All rights reserved. No part of this book may be reproduced without written permission from the publisher. Printed and bound in the United States of America.

Printing   1   2   3   4   5   6   7   8   9

Library of Congress Cataloging-in-Publication Data
Koosmann, Melissa.
The fall of apartheid in South Africa / by Melissa Koosmann.
   p. cm. — (Monumental milestones)
Includes bibliographical references and index.
ISBN 978-1-58415-736-6 (library bound)
1. Apartheid—South Africa—History—Juvenile literature. 2. Anti-apartheid
   movements—South Africa—History—Juvenile literature. 3. Post-apartheid era—
   South Africa—Juvenile literature. 4. South Africa—Race relations— History—
   Juvenile literature. 5. South Africa—Politics and government—1994— —Juvenile
   literature. I. Title.
DT1757.K67 2010
968.06—dc22

                                                                        2009027324

ABOUT THE AUTHOR: Melissa Koosmann studied creative writing at Linfield College and the University of Arizona. She spent several years teaching English and working with students with learning disabilities. In April 2008, she and her husband moved to Cape Town, South Africa, where she tutors at a local elementary school.

PUBLISHER'S NOTE: This story is based on the author's extensive research, which she believes to be accurate. Documentation of such research is contained on page 46.
   The internet sites referenced herein were active as of the publication date. Due to the fleeting nature of some web sites, we cannot guarantee they will all be active when you are reading this book.

MONUMENTAL MILESTONES
GREAT EVENTS OF MODERN TIMES

Contents

*For Your Information

The day after his release, Nelson Mandela held his youngest grandchild, Bambata, in his arms.

After twenty-seven years in prison, Nelson Mandela was eager to spend time with his family. However, political duties often took him away from home. He spent the next ten years working to build and lead a new, democratic South Africa.

No Easy Journey

In Nelson Mandela's first hour of freedom, he was already late. A huge crowd was waiting in the South African city of Cape Town, thirty-five miles away, to hear him speak. But he was stuck at the gates of Victor Verster Prison.

A crowd of reporters surrounded Mandela, their cameras clicking and flashing. One of them shoved something long and dark in Mandela's face. Mandela flinched, thinking the strange object might be a weapon. It was only a microphone.[1]

On February 11, 1990, after twenty-seven years in prison, Mandela was returning to a different world. He had fought his whole life to end an oppressive system of laws called apartheid (uh-PART-hide), which kept black South Africans like him living in poverty and fear. For decades, people of all races had protested against these laws. Now, for the first time, the apartheid government was listening. Nelson Mandela was walking out of prison, and most South Africans hoped he would lead their country to freedom.

After Mandela separated himself from the reporters, his driver took him along back roads away from the jail. When they heard on the radio that Mandela was coming, white farmers who lived on these roads ran out to watch him pass. Some of them raised their fists in the official salute of Mandela's organization, the African National Congress.

Mandela was amazed to see these white farmers showing support for black rights in public. He knew this took great courage, because some of their neighbors surely wanted to keep apartheid in place. These neighbors might resort to violence against those who disagreed with them. Mandela stopped to thank some of these supporters for their bravery.[2]

Meanwhile, in Cape Town, the crowd was getting restless.

The Crowd

Thousands of people waited in front of the Cape Town City Hall. Most of them—the blacks, Indians, and mixed-race people South Africans call coloureds—had been suffering under apartheid all their lives. Over the past few years, many had attended protests and seen police fire guns into crowds. Some had run with defiant mobs, looting stores and burning buildings. Today, most of them probably weren't sure the government would allow Mandela to speak.

As the hours stretched on, impatient people on the edges of the crowd began to riot. They broke shop windows and stole the goods inside. The police released tear gas to stop them. Somewhere, gunshots rang out. Many people fled the scene in terror as organizers and police tried to restore order. In spite of the violence, about 100,000 people stayed.[3] No matter how scary it got, they would wait to see Mandela.

Finally a convoy of cars appeared, and there he was! The people nearby could see him through the lead car's windows. He was an old man now, with white hair and a lined face, but he was still Mandela. The crowd cheered.

Then Mandela's driver did something strange. Instead of steering around the edge of the crowd, he drove straight in. People ran up and surrounded the car so tightly on all sides that it had to stop. It couldn't move forward, and it couldn't go back. Mandela was trapped!

In their excitement, people shook Mandela's car and banged on the windows and the hood. Some of them even jumped on top. Inside, it sounded like a vicious hailstorm. For more than an hour, the people vented their hope on the man who had inspired it.

Mandela was afraid the people might accidentally kill him, but he didn't let his face show fear. He sat still, holding up his thumb to show his respect.

The driver was terrified, too. He tried to get out of the car, but he couldn't open his door against the crush of bodies. By the time a group of marshals cleared a path so that he could back out, he was in a panic. He drove away from the crowd as fast as he could.

"Man, where are you going?" Mandela asked.

"I don't know!" said the driver, and he kept on driving.[4]

Amandla!

The crowd wondered where Mandela had gone. Would he be allowed to speak? Had the Prime Minister changed his mind and thrown him back in prison?

"We want Nelson! We want Nelson!" the crowd shouted.

"Comrades!" yelled an organizer. "He has waited twenty-seven years for his freedom! We have stood here for five or six hours. Where is our patience?"[5]

But the people were tired of being patient. They shouted and shoved, and some of them began rioting all over again. It was beginning to look as if the day would dissolve into violence.

Mandela convinced his driver to take him back to City Hall just in time. The man dropped him off at the back of the building, where the crowd wasn't as thick. Organizers rushed Mandela up to the top floor and out onto a balcony.

When they caught sight of their leader, the crowd let out a deafening cheer. Mandela raised his fist. "*Amandla* [ah-MAAHN-dlah]!" he shouted. "Power!"

Near the end of apartheid, children in the township of Soweto saw many protests. *Amandla*, which means "power," was an important rallying cry.

At Mandela's first speech, people scrambled to get close to him.

The people saw Mandela as their best chance for a new democracy. Although he spent many years suffering under the apartheid regime, he did not show bitterness. He ended this speech with the words, "I thank you."

"*Ngawethu* [ah-WAAY-too]!" the crowd responded. "Belongs to the people!"[6]

This chant was the people's way of demanding a voice in their country's government. Many of them, like Mandela, had risked everything to fight for a democratic South Africa. They had not reached this goal yet, but Mandela's release made it seem possible they someday would.

In the speech that followed, Mandela spoke about the future of South Africa. He said that apartheid must end, but he urged the people to resolve their problems peacefully. Instead of violence between whites and blacks, he called for equal rights for all.[7] He wanted to show that South Africans could end apartheid without going to war.

But could they? On the day Mandela was released, nobody knew for sure—not even Mandela himself.

Apartheid reigned in South Africa for a little more than forty years, from 1948 to the early 1990s, but the roots of this oppressive system took hold much earlier. Shortly after the Dutch built their first colony in southern Africa in 1652, the white settlers began fighting with the black Africans over land and resources. This fighting flared up many times over the next two hundred years. Both sides won many battles, but the settlers, who could always bring more guns and soldiers from Europe, ended up in control.

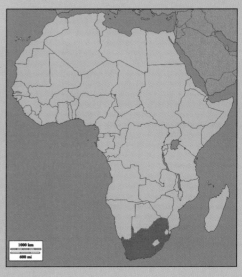

South Africa covers the southern tip of the African continent.

The early white settlers had children and grandchildren who regarded Africa as their home. They called themselves Afrikaners, which means "Africans" in Dutch, and they believed God wanted them to develop and control the land. In order to do this, they fought not only black Africans, but also some of the white settlers who arrived after them. In particular, they struggled for independence from the English, who controlled southern Africa for many years.

Over time, black people began to participate in the white economy, starting their own farms and businesses. Many white people, both English and Afrikaners, felt threatened by black successes. White workers thought they deserved higher wages than black workers, and white farmers and mine owners needed cheap black labor in order to make a profit. They asked their leaders to stop black people from taking away what they believed was rightfully theirs.

Time and time again, white South African leaders did what their people demanded. They made laws that kept black people from holding high-status jobs, and they declared that whites had to be paid more than blacks for the same work. They refused to let black people own land outside certain areas, and they forced black travelers to carry special identity papers.

All these laws were in place before apartheid. Apartheid made them worse.[8]

Black people faced constant humiliation. As this caution sign shows, some whites regarded blacks as less than human.

In a sports arena in the city of Bloe...
divided the sections for blacks and wh...

The apartheid system kept
people separated in every
sphere of life. Segregation
rules were so strong that it was
nearly impossible for blacks
and whites to get to know each
other.

Building Apartheid

In 1948, the Afrikaners felt their culture was under attack. On one side, English leaders controlled the South African government, often making choices the Afrikaners disliked. On the other side, black South Africans were moving to the cities, getting jobs, and fighting for better rights. Black people have always made up the majority of South Africa's population. As they gained more power, the Afrikaners worried black people might take control.[1]

It was nearly time for the 1948 elections, and the Afrikaner-dominated National Party was working hard to get votes. National Party leaders campaigned on a platform of undisguised racism, using slogans like "The white man must always be boss." The voters were all white. Some of them were offended by this message, but enough of them responded to it. The National Party won by a narrow margin.[2]

As soon as they had power, the National Party brought all of South Africa's unjust racial laws together and molded them into one strict code to ensure white supremacy. This code was called apartheid, which literally means "apartness." Its main goal was to keep all of South Africa's differently colored people separate.

To do this, the new leaders created separate schools, buses, and neighborhoods for people of the different races. They reserved more jobs for whites than ever before, and they put together a population register that labeled all South Africans by race. They outlawed marriage between people of different races, including marriages that already existed.[3] Under the new laws, some parents could not even legally live with their mixed-race children.[4]

Life Under Apartheid

Beauty Qabela lived in a village on a small land reserve called a homeland, which the South African government had set aside for her tribe. There were almost no jobs in her village, so she couldn't earn money. The land was overcrowded, so her family couldn't grow enough food to support itself. If Qabela didn't go away to find work, her grandmother and nine brothers and sisters would starve.

Qabela moved to Johannesburg, one of South Africa's biggest cities. This was a risky thing to do. Because she was black, she wasn't allowed to leave home without a document called a pass that said who she was and for whom she worked. Qabela's pass showed clearly that she had no job and no right to be in Johannesburg. She knew she could go to prison for traveling without permission, but she had no other choice.

When she got to Johannesburg, she made her way to a neighborhood where black workers lived. Such neighborhoods were called townships, and like the homelands, they were severely overcrowded. They barely had enough space to house the workers who were legally employed; they were filled to bursting with

Children in the homeland village of Ekuvukeni pose for a rare chance to be photographed.

In Ekuvukeni, barbed wire separated blacks from whites. Some black children saw almost no white people except for the police officers and public officials who tormented their families.

desperate people like Qabela who moved in illegally. Few township residents had electricity or running water. As many as ten or fifteen people might share a house with only one or two rooms.

In the townships, black people like Qabela lived in constant fear. Theft and violence plagued the streets, but the police did little to protect the victims. Instead, they made regular raids on township homes, arresting all adults who could not prove they were employed.[5]

A black person's passbook. This document was sometimes called a *dompass* or "stupid pass" because black people were considered unintelligent.

Even after she found work, Qabela knew she could go to jail any time she left her pass at home or failed to update it properly. One day, while she was out buying groceries for her employers, a police officer stopped her. Qabela's boss had forgotten to sign her pass, so the officer put her in handcuffs and led her away.

The judge spent only five minutes on Qabela's trial. He pronounced her guilty and gave her a choice: She could pay a fine of 30 rand (about $10) or serve a 15-day jail sentence. Qabela could not afford the fine, so she went to prison. When she got out, the police sent her back to her village.

Qabela was glad to see her family, but her village was a sad place. The people worked hard in the fields, but they never produced enough. The land was wearing away from overuse, so farmers produced less and less food every year. Most families no longer lived together. The fathers and many of the mothers were away in Johannesburg, working to support their families. Children grew up with just one parent, with a grandparent, or with no adults to care for them at all.

Qabela did the only thing she could do. She went back to Johannesburg. She found another job and worked until she was caught again and forced back home. In all, she was arrested and sent back to her homeland ten times.[6]

Bantu Education

Under apartheid, children of each race had to go to separate schools. The government spent the most money on white schools, and it declared that different information must be taught to each race. According to Hendrik Verwoerd (fayr-VERD), the first minister of Bantu (BAN-too) Education under apartheid, schooling "must train and teach people in accordance with their opportunities in life."[7] In other words, black children could only grow up to be servants and laborers, so there was no point in teaching them to be anything more.

Within the Bantu Education system, black students were taught the basics of reading, writing, and math. They were also taught how to be clean and obedient. Teachers were poorly paid and poorly trained, and classes were overcrowded.

The law said that black children had to go to school until they were fourteen, but officials did not enforce this rule. Many children dropped out, for dozens of reasons. Sometimes they couldn't afford school fees, or they needed to work to help support their families. Some of them simply hated the system and quit in protest.[8]

Black schools were terribly overcrowded.

Under the Bantu Education system, many kids never managed to learn basic skills such as reading and writing. When they became adults, this made it nearly impossible for them to get good jobs—even after apartheid laws were repealed.

Of all the policies of apartheid, Bantu Education may have been the most debilitating. It produced a workforce that could not do the jobs the country needed to have done. South Africa continues to cope with the problems it created by not educating its people equally.

Apartheid and White South Africans

While apartheid left black people like Beauty Qabela living in desperation, it benefited white South Africans. A constant stream of cheap black labor flowed into the cities, which helped white businesses make money. White homeowners had more free time because they could hire black maids and nannies. If black workers asked for time off or higher wages, their employers could easily fire them and hire others. Many whites felt conflicted about apartheid, but for forty years, a majority continued voting for the National Party.

People of different races had to ride separate buses. Black buses came less often, even though more black people than white relied on public transportation.

WHITE PERSONS ONLY

NET BLANKES

STORTE DENS
TOILET

Only people with white skin were allowed to enjoy the beautiful sand and sea at this beach in Strandfontein.

Because blacks and whites had so little opportunity to get to know each other, they also had little chance to learn to understand and respect each other.

During apartheid, few white South Africans knew very much about the lives of the black people in their country. The government pressured the newspapers to make apartheid policies sound reasonable, so it was hard to get truthful information. White people rarely saw black townships and homelands for themselves. As late as 1982, nearly 3 out of 4 white South Africans said they thought the black people in their country were happy with their lives.[9]

Still, it was possible for white people to see the truth and find the courage to do something about it. A few white people dedicated their lives to fighting apartheid. One of them, Helen Joseph, fought apartheid tirelessly for forty years. She endured imprisonment and house arrest for the cause, and she was even the victim of several assassination attempts.[10]

Writers played a vital role in raising awareness of apartheid's cruel treatment of black South Africans. *Cry, the Beloved Country* by Alan Paton is one of the best-known novels on the subject. Published in 1948, it was one of the first stories to create an honest depiction of the desperate circumstances of life for black South Africans. Paton also portrays the complicated feelings that black and white South Africans held about the relations between races in their country.

Over the next few decades, many brave writers published stories, novels, and poems that challenged people around the world to imagine life under apartheid. Some of their books inspired people outside South Africa to protest apartheid and to raise money to help South Africa's oppressed people. Two of the most influential South African writers, Nadine Gordimer and J.M. Coetzee, later received Nobel Prizes for literature.[11]

A few small newspapers refused to publish the news from the government's point of view. The government frowned on the publication of stories about the black resistance and forbade newspapers to print the words or pictures of antiapartheid leaders. Journalists who disobeyed these rules risked their jobs and their safety, but a

In 1982, *The Star* newspaper reported on a government plan to give territory—and the people who lived there—to Swaziland. Nobody consulted the one million black people whose lives would have been changed by this measure.

few of them did it anyway. Editors of a newspaper called the *Rand Daily Mail* were repeatedly sued or fired for upsetting apartheid leaders. This paper was internationally recognized for revealing the truth to those South Africans who wanted to read it.[12]

During the Defiance Campaign, ordinary professionals, laborers, and housewives went to jail for their beliefs.

For more than forty years, brave South Africans of every race made personal sacrifices to fight the apartheid regime. Often it seemed that no positive end to their struggle would be possible.

The Fight for Freedom

On June 26, 1952, in a town called Port Elizabeth, thirty-three people walked into a train station. Their friends and families stood by to cheer them on. They used a Whites Only entrance, but they were not white. They were black, coloured, and Indian. As they stepped through the door, police officers arrested them and led them away.

Later that day, outside Johannesburg, a crowd walked into a township without permits. Then a group of black people marched through the streets after their eleven P.M. curfew. The police took them all to jail.

These brave people were volunteering for the Defiance Campaign, the first countrywide antiapartheid protest, which was organized by the African National Congress (ANC) in cooperation with several other resistance groups. By breaking laws and serving jail time, Defiance Campaign volunteers called attention to the injustice of the apartheid system. To emphasize their point, the volunteers remained absolutely peaceful. Sometimes they even called the police ahead of time to let them know when and where they were going to defy the law.

The Defiance Campaign caught the country's attention and brought people together to fight apartheid. South Africans were inspired to see ordinary people making personal sacrifices to support the cause. Across the country, people of all races joined peaceful marches to support volunteers who had been jailed.[1]

But the apartheid regime did not change any of its unjust laws. Instead, it cracked down on the protesters as serious criminals. Many of the Defiance Campaign's leaders were banned, which meant they could not attend meetings or leave the towns where they lived. These restrictions applied to their whole lives, not just their political activities. A banning order once made it illegal for Nelson Mandela to attend his son's birthday party.[2]

The Freedom Charter

South Africa's government did not represent the majority of its people. In 1955, antiapartheid groups joined together to write down a vision of the government most South Africans really wanted. They sent out flyers to ask for ideas from people of every race and region of South Africa. City dwellers and farmers, sports groups and students all mailed in their suggestions. They wrote them on the backs of flyers, on notebook paper, and even on napkins. Most of them said that every adult in South Africa should have the right to vote.

With the people's ideas in hand, antiapartheid leaders wrote a document called the Freedom Charter. It began with the following words:

> We, the people of South Africa, declare for all our country and the world to know: that South Africa belongs to all who live in it, black and white, and that no government can justly claim authority unless it is based on the will of the people.[3]

The apartheid government considered these words to be treason.

When they finished writing the Freedom Charter, antiapartheid leaders held an event called the Congress of the People. On June 25 and 26, 1955, three thousand South Africans of every skin color came together to celebrate. They talked, ate, and sang freedom songs. All around them, signs proclaimed: FREEDOM IN OUR LIFETIME, LONG LIVE THE STRUGGLE. They tried to ignore the police officers lurking at the edges of the crowd.

At the Congress of the People, antiapartheid leaders read the Freedom Charter out loud. The crowd cheered at the end of each section. When the reading was finished, the leaders called for a vote to approve the document.

Before the vote could be counted, police rushed onto the stage. They surrounded the crowds to prevent people from leaving. They seized every document they could find, even signs from the food table that said SOUP WITH MEAT and SOUP WITHOUT MEAT. After that, they wrote down the names of all the participants and sent them home.[4]

Even though the police broke up the party, resistance groups considered the Congress of the People a success. Now they shared a vision of a concrete, positive goal for the future of South Africa: freedom and equality for people of all races.[5]

The government charged the leaders of the Congress of the People with treason and held a public trial. In court, lawyers tried to prove that the congress leaders were dangerous communists who were trying to bring down the government. The trial lasted five years, but the government's lawyers could not convince the judge. In 1961, in a decision that embarrassed apartheid leaders, the judge found all of the defendants not guilty.[6]

Massacre!

The apartheid regime continued to regard protesters as criminals, but the people kept trying to push for justice. On March 21, 1960, thousands of people across the country assembled to protest laws that required black people to carry passes.

In the township of Sharpeville, a crowd gathered in front of the police station. Organizers from a group called the Pan Africanist Congress (PAC) moved through the crowd, reminding people to remain peaceful.[7] The protesters obeyed

On March 21, 1960, people around the world were shocked by the Sharpeville Massacre. Today, March 21 is the International Day for the Elimination of Racial Discrimination.

Thousands mourned the victims of the Sharpeville Massacre.

the organizers, but some thought the police looked nervous. There were only seventy-five officers to deal with the thousands of people in the crowd.[8]

Humphrey Tyler, a journalist who was covering the event, reported that everyone acted peaceful and friendly. "Afrika!" the crowd members shouted, laughing as they held up their thumbs in a freedom salute.[9]

Suddenly, near the police, Tyler thought the people's shouts sounded different. He heard a machine gun fire. Some of the women in the crowd started to laugh. They thought the police were shooting blanks.

They were shooting real bullets. They made no warnings or threats. They simply opened fire. People panicked and fled in all directions, and the police kept shooting. Tyler saw a little boy holding his jacket up over his head as if it might block the bullets.[10] Sixty-nine people—children and adults—died that day, and 186 others were wounded. Most of those people were shot in the back.[11]

The Resistance Turns to Violence

After Sharpeville, the ANC organized a national day of mourning, encouraging people to burn their passes in public. But apartheid leaders did not back down. Instead, they declared a state of emergency and placed the country under martial law. They gave themselves the power to arrest anyone engaging in protests,[12] and they outlawed the ANC and PAC. People could now go to prison just for belonging to these groups.[13]

These new laws crippled the resistance. Most ANC and PAC leaders fled the country. The few who stayed realized that they could no longer make progress by resisting peacefully. It seemed clear that the government was never going to change of its own free will. Apartheid leaders were willing to shoot or imprison anyone who tried to resist them. In the face of that kind of brutality, resistance groups either had to give up or fight back.[14]

They chose to fight back. Some groups committed gruesome murders and deadly terrorist attacks.[15] Nelson Mandela and the ANC started an armed wing whose mission was to sabotage the government. They bombed power plants and similar targets, but they carefully avoided killing people. They named their group Umkhonto we Sizwe (oom-KOHN-toh-way-SEEZ-way), which means "the Spear of Africa."[16]

Mandela lived on the run, staying with friends and allies. Sometimes he lived in white neighborhoods, where he had to stay indoors all day with the blinds drawn so that nobody would see him. Sometimes he posed as a gardener or waiter. During this time, Mandela recruited helpers and read dozens of books about military and armed resistance.[17]

Mandela was trying to build the beginnings of an army. After many years, he hoped Umkhonto we Sizwe would be able to fight the South African military face to face and force the apartheid leaders to step down. He never got that far. On August 5, 1962, he was arrested and thrown into prison for minor offenses such as organizing strikes and leaving the country illegally. Soon, the other major leaders of Umkhonto we Sizwe were caught too. The government put them all on trial for their lives.[18]

A Brave Dare

On October 9, 1963, the first day of the Rivonia Trial, as the trial of Umkhonto we Sizwe's leaders came to be known, guards brought Mandela and nine other accused prisoners into the courtroom. As each one entered, he turned to face the crowd and raised his fist in the ANC salute.

In spite of the small victory they won in avoiding the death penalty, many years of hardship were in store for Mandela and his fellow prisoners. Their country and their families faced the hardship of getting along without them.

On their way to Robben Island Prison, the leaders of Umkhonto we Sizwe remained defiant, raising their fists to show their resolve.

"Amandla! . . .Ngawethu!" the ANC's supporters chanted.[19]

Although they acted defiant, the prisoners knew the situation was serious. They were on trial for sabotage and conspiracy against the government. If they lost, they would probably face a sentence of death by hanging.[20]

The prisoners decided to admit they had broken laws. They argued that the apartheid government deserved to be on trial, not them. At the beginning of his defense, Mandela explained this in a speech. He accepted responsibility for his actions, pointed to the government as the criminals, and said he would give anything for the ideal of a free society. At the end of the speech, he looked straight at the judge and said, "It is an ideal for which I am prepared to die."[21]

In a way, Mandela was daring the judge to sentence him to die. He was showing that he was proud of what he had done, and that he had done it out of a sense of justice. After that day, the judge never looked Mandela in the eye again. The Rivonia Trial ended with a guilty verdict, but the judge did not sentence the prisoners to die. Instead, he sentenced them to life in prison.[22]

Mandela and the others were taken to Robben Island, a prison off the South African coast. They were forced to spend their days doing hard labor, cut off from their families and from the resistance. They were among the last resistance leaders who had stayed in the country, so their conviction was a huge blow to their cause. Umkhonto we Sizwe and the ANC, along with other resistance groups, continued in exile only. Little resistance could continue within the borders of South Africa for many years. The struggle was nearly crushed. It looked like the apartheid government had won.

However, without knowing it, the government was planting the seeds of a new phase of resistance. The next generation of black South African children grew up without any resistance leaders around them. They knew that the government would stop at nothing to keep black people down. As they grew into their teenage years, they became angry and bitter. They vowed to destroy the apartheid regime at all costs. These teens led the last chapter of the resistance.

Those who participated in the Congress of the People believed that South Africans should work toward equality for people of all races. They were fighting for a "rainbow nation" in which people of every skin color could live together in harmony. But not all antiapartheid groups fought for this goal. Many activists believed that only black people had the right to run the country. They thought that if all the races tried to live side by side, white people would always demand a dominant role.

In 1959, a group of leaders broke away from the ANC and formed the PAC. These leaders felt that South Africa should be a country of, by, and for black Africans. In their view, everyone else was an unwelcome foreigner. The PAC gained a great deal of popular support and brought many people into the antiapartheid struggle. However, they developed a rivalry with the ANC. The PAC sometimes worked harder to weaken the ANC than to end apartheid.[23]

After the government banned the ANC and PAC, a movement called Black Consciousness grew up in the townships and homelands. Black Consciousness emphasized pride in black culture. It played a vital role in helping many young black South Africans understand the value of their culture. However, Black Consciousness leaders rejected the help of like-minded people from other racial groups.[24]

Another black political group, the Inkatha (in-KAH-thuh) Freedom Party (IFP), agreed with some apartheid principles. They thought it was okay to keep people of different cultures separate. The IFP began in an area that was dominated by the Zulu tribe. The leader of the party, Chief Buthelezi (boo-tuh-LAY-zee), wanted to create a separate and powerful Zulu nation. If that was not possible, he wanted to secure special rights for Zulus within a multiracial South Africa. When it became clear that apartheid was ending, Chief Buthelezi and the IFP joined forces with radical white Afrikaner groups who shared their vision of power for minority groups within South Africa.[25] The disagreements between groups like these led to a great deal of violence among black South Africans, as well as between blacks and whites, even as apartheid neared its end.

Bystanders flee tear gas set off by the police during a violent clash between the ANC and the IFP. During the transition period at the end of apartheid, such events were frighteningly common.

Angry because police had gunned
demonstrators, rioters burned a bus ar
destruction at the Soweto uprising.

The 1976 protest in Soweto
began as a peaceful, well-
organized student walkout on
June 16. The students were
protesting a petty law. Nobody
expected the police to open fire
on crowds of children.

Apartheid Falls Apart

On June 16, 1976, most children in Soweto (soh-WEH-toh), a group of townships near Johannesburg, went to school expecting a normal day.[1] Normal, for black children like them, meant attending classes that had nearly 60 students for every teacher. The government spent about one sixteenth as much money for each black student as it spent for each white student.[2] Black teachers were overworked, poorly trained, and underpaid. Some of them did not know there were other ways to keep their classes under control besides beating and humiliating the students. With so few resources, even the best teachers could not teach very well.[3]

By this time, the white Minister of Bantu Education had declared that half of all classes at black schools must be taught in Afrikaans, the language of the Afrikaners. This angered the students—indeed, the whole black community. Afrikaans, to them, was the language of their oppressors. A few students joined the growing Black Consciousness movement and decided to raise a protest.[4]

At the beginning of the school day, student organizers spread the word, and a march began. Youngsters walked from several different high schools toward a central meeting point. They stopped by other schools and encouraged more students to join them on the way. As the crowd grew, it became quite rowdy, but as usual, leaders worked hard to keep it peaceful. One leader, a boy named Tsietsi Mashinini, climbed onto a tractor so that he could speak to the crowd.

"Brothers and sisters," he shouted, "I appeal to you—keep calm and cool. We have just received a report that the police are coming. Don't taunt them, don't do anything to them. Be cool and calm. We are not fighting."[5]

The crowd was growing larger than anyone had expected. As many as 10,000 people, including some parents and teachers, marched along, singing freedom songs and shouting. When police prevented them from marching further, everyone stood still, raising their fists and voices.

A white policeman raised his revolver and shot into the crowd.

Four children were shot. The others screamed and ran. People started throwing rocks. They set fire to cars and buildings, looted stores, and attacked white officials. Soon whole sections of Soweto were in flames.

People join protests for various reasons. In Soweto that day, the protesters were students who cared deeply about improving black rights, and some of them wanted to vent their anger. When the violence erupted, many tried to run somewhere safe.[6]

There was no safe place for them. By the time the riot was in full force, police were shooting and beating students at apparent random. Inside the houses that were not in flames, people huddled with their families, hoping the bullets would not penetrate the thin walls. Younger students, who had not joined the protests, ran home from school in terror, coughing and vomiting from the tear gas in the air.[7]

At the end of the day, the government-controlled news reported that 23 children had been killed. Other sources guessed that as many as 200 were actually dead.[8] And it was not over. During the next few days, students kept clashing with

Students begin their protest in Soweto.

Faced with internal chaos and international pressure, apartheid leaders slowly began making changes.

police. In the most unstable areas, persistent riots kept schools closed for months.[9]

After the Soweto riots, some students fled South Africa. They sneaked across the border into other African countries, where they joined military camps and trained to be soldiers for the ANC and PAC.[10] When adults said they should be in school, they chanted their new slogan: "Freedom now, education later." These teens played a vital role in the shift to a democratic South Africa, but many of them received no education at all.[11]

The Death of Biko

Even before the Soweto riots, the apartheid government stopped trying to pretend they were offering protesters fair trials under the law. The government gave police the power to hold protesters for up to ninety days without trial. These prisoners sometimes died in jail, and the reasons police stated for these deaths often seemed unlikely. Officers claimed one prisoner died after he fell down the stairs. They said another was killed when he slipped on a piece of soap. When concerned people challenged these explanations in the courts, judges accepted the bizarre police explanations for the deaths.[12]

In 1977, Black Consciousness leader Stephen (Steve) Biko was arrested and held without trial under South Africa's ninety-day detention law. He died while in custody. Biko was well known, so many people wanted to know what happened to him. Police claimed that he had starved himself during a hunger strike. But journalists for the *Rand Daily Mail* interviewed a doctor who had examined Biko's body. They found out he had died because of injuries he suffered when a police officer beat him during questioning. They reported as much of the story as they safely could, and the country was shocked. As usual, the courts declared that the officers involved were not to blame. This decision caused an outcry across South Africa and around the world.[13]

Biko's death added more momentum to the fight against apartheid. In particular, it increased the anger of his followers, who vowed to make South Africa impossible to govern.

Stephen Biko

Life in the 1980s

In the 1980s, riots became commonplace in black neighborhoods. Police continued shooting and killing protesters. Protesters, meanwhile, attacked anyone connected with the apartheid government. In particular, they lashed out against people they called "system blacks"—black people who worked as teachers, police officers, and officials under the apartheid system. Sometimes the mobs murdered such people. Nobody was safe from being labeled a traitor, including the leaders of the protests.

For ordinary black South Africans, these riots made life harder than before. Many lost their jobs because they had trouble getting to and from work. They constantly struggled to earn enough money to buy food and other necessities. Many refused to take part in the resistance because they wanted nothing to do with the violence.

Not everyone had the choice to stay out of the struggle. Miriam Mathabane was a teenager in a township called Alexandra in the 1980s. She wanted to stay out of the riots and get an education. But one day a group of teenaged Black Consciousness leaders came into her school and forced everyone out of class. "Either you join us or you're against us," one of them shouted. Not wanting to be killed for being a "system black," Mathabane marched and shouted with the others until she had a chance to slip away.

Rioters destroyed property to vent their anger against the oppressive regime.

After that day, Mathabane's school stayed closed for months, and she was forced to join protests almost every night. The government imposed martial law but could not get the streets under control. Police massacres of rioters became weekly news. More than 900 South Africans died in violence related to political unrest that year.[14]

Black Consciousness leaders achieved their goal of making South Africa impossible to control. To do this, they risked everything—including not only their own lives, but also the lives of everyone in their communities.

Pressure, Politics, and the Prisoner

Apartheid was falling apart. The riots raging in the townships would not stop. Outside the country, world leaders
were pressuring the South African government to end
apartheid. They banned South Africa from international
sporting events. They also refused to trade with the apartheid regime. This left the apartheid government with little
money to run the country.[15]

In the face of these problems, apartheid leaders
finally began to see the need to change. Prime Minister
Pieter Willem Botha got rid of what he called "petty
apartheid," the separate public facilities and the signs that
declared certain areas Whites Only. His government gave
limited voting rights to coloured and Indian citizens and
granted blacks the right to form trade unions.[16]

Nelson Mandela
mends clothes in the
prison yard. In prison,
antiapartheid leaders
were forced to do
menial labor.

None of these small improvements made much
difference. Pressure from other countries continued. Coloured and Indian people resented the limitations on their
voting rights, and most of them chose to protest by not
voting at all. The riots quieted at times and then flared up
again. It seemed likely that the country would descend
into civil war.[17]

Nelson Mandela saw all this from prison, and he realized that war would
destroy South Africa. The resistance did not have a big enough army to beat the
South African military, but the white minority was too small to overwhelm the
black majority. He believed that if a war started, it would drag on for years and
cause suffering for everyone. In 1982, Mandela had been moved to a prison on
the mainland, near Cape Town. He convinced the last two Prime Ministers of the
apartheid regime, Botha and Frederik Willem de Klerk, to meet with him for secret
talks. He tried to persuade them that black and white South Africans had to make
peace.

To everyone's surprise, Prime Minister de Klerk finally listened. In a his-
toric speech on February 2, 1990, he took the first steps to dismantle apartheid.
He announced that he would allow the ANC and PAC to operate, free the political
prisoners, and lift several restrictions on people's freedoms. Nine days later, Nelson

Mandela walked out of prison. Negotiations for a new, democratic South Africa were about to begin.[18]

Negotiations

In May 1990, the ANC and the apartheid government began meeting to talk about future negotiations for a democratic constitution. These "talks about talks" were plagued by mistrust. After forty years of apartheid, it was hard for people on either side to believe that the other wanted to make peace.

During this time, the violence got worse instead of better. Both black and white extremists resorted to terrorism. They set off bombs, shot at people in restaurants and bars, and attacked people at political rallies. Bombings and shootings occurred in white neighborhoods as well as black ones. The whole country lived in constant fear.

During the first few years of the 1990s, every major political group in the country was accused of violent wrongdoing, including the ANC and de Klerk's government. The ANC agreed to stop its armed struggle, but mistrust continued. In a scandal that nearly ended the peace process, Mandela accused the government of permitting attacks on his party's members. He pulled out of the talks until he and de Klerk signed a Record of Understanding stating that the police had to protect ANC supporters.[19]

Even when violence did not stop the negotiations, disagreements slowed them down. Although de Klerk was willing to allow blacks to vote, he still wanted whites to have extra power. The ANC refused to accept anything short of absolute equality, and the PAC wanted a black government only. In a complicated twist, the Inkatha Freedom Party sided with white Afrikaner groups, calling for special rights for both the Zulu and Afrikaner minorities.

In spite of all the problems, negotiations slowly progressed. The government repealed the last apartheid laws. Leaders came to agree on the way a new government should be run. A majority of white South Africans voted to support reform, and countries around the world resumed trading with South Africa.

By 1993, leaders had made enough progress to set a date for South Africa's first free election. They ratified an interim constitution and set up a council of leaders to govern the country until elections could take place. People around the world applauded South Africa for avoiding an all-out war, and Mandela and de Klerk jointly received a Nobel Peace Prize for leading their country into democracy.[20]

While young people protested in the streets, Nelson Mandela and many of the other older leaders of the antiapartheid struggle spent decades locked away in Robben Island prison. These leaders didn't stay idle while others did their work in the outside world. They continued the antiapartheid struggle in jail.

The prisoners on Robben Island fought hard to make the guards treat all prisoners equally. With patient effort over several years, they secured the same food rations and privileges for prisoners of all races. They also won the right to study, and some of them earned degrees from universities around the world. In this way, they managed to gain some of the knowledge and skills they knew they would need if they were ever freed.[21]

As years passed, more and more young people served prison terms on Robben Island. The older prisoners, including Mandela, noticed that many of their younger companions knew little about the history of racial struggle in southern Africa. They decided to develop classes and teach the newcomers about their common past.

While he was imprisoned on Robben Island, Nelson Mandela (left) held a discussion with his close friend and fellow prisoner, Walter Sisulu. Sisulu later became deputy president of the ANC.

On most days at Robben Island, the political prisoners worked together in a lime quarry. They passed the time by holding school while they worked. In the morning, the men in each "class" would gather around their "teacher." They all dug in the lime and listened as the teacher talked. In this way, they learned about their history without breaking prison rules.[22]

Nonpolitical prisoners lived separately from the political prisoners, but Mandela and his friends managed to teach them, too. They sent notes back and forth inside matchboxes and with food deliveries. They even smuggled lessons by taping them inside toilet bowls.[23]

People who passed in and out of the prison on short sentences took the knowledge they gained at Robben Island back to South Africa's cities and towns. Some South Africans began calling Robben Island prison "The University."

In 1994, an elderly black woman cast he
the township of Edendale, outside Piet

The first multiracial election
ended in a clear victory for
antiapartheid groups. The
ANC received more than
12 million votes, over four
times as many as the National
Party.

CHAPTER 5

Democracy

On April 27, 1994, South Africa held its first free election. Everyone was afraid terrorists would attack the polling places, but fear didn't keep voters at home. People turned out in huge numbers to cast their ballots. Some of the lines stretched three miles (five kilometers). Voters had to wait for up to seven hours without food, water, or bathrooms.[1] Most were very patient. To everyone's relief, there was not a single act of violence at any voting station.[2]

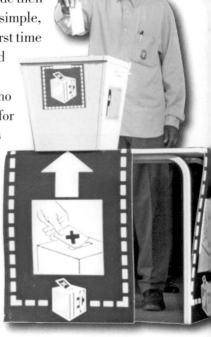

When voters got to the front of the line, they picked up a slip of paper. They had to write an X in a little square next to the picture of the leader for whom they were voting. When they'd made their mark, they slipped the paper into a box. The process was simple, but for the vast majority of South Africans, this was the first time they had had such power. Some people broke down and cried after they slipped their ballots into the box.[3]

In that first election, there were a few people who tried to steal ballot boxes or stuff them with extra votes for their favorite party.[4] But for the most part, the process went smoothly. Surprisingly, in a country where many people could not read and most had never voted before, less than 1 percent of ballots were spoiled. The Independent Electoral Commission declared the election free and fair.[5]

When the ballots were counted, it became clear that the ANC had won by a landslide. Nelson Mandela became the country's first president under representative democratic rule.

People called it a miracle. At long last, apartheid was really over.

Mandela casting his vote

Truth and Reconciliation

Apartheid caused suffering that could not simply be forgotten, but its leaders had agreed to change in the end. Because of this, South Africa's new leaders could not just throw the old ones in prison. In fact, they needed the old leaders to help them run the country. But the people of South Africa needed a way to heal from the wrongs of their past.

Leaders formed a committee called the Truth and Reconciliation Commission (TRC). In some ways, the TRC was like a court. It would hear confessions of people who hurt and killed others under apartheid's rule. The commission could pardon people who confessed, on two conditions: They had to tell the whole truth about the crimes they committed, and they had to prove that they had performed their acts for political reasons.

But the TRC was also far more than a court. It was designed to hear from the people who suffered under apartheid, too. The stories and confessions were broadcast on national television so that everyone in South Africa could listen. This process gave the entire country a way to admit the wrongs of the past, and it recorded that history so that the experiences of apartheid would not be forgotten.

Most South Africans found it painful to listen to the stories that came out at the TRC hearings. People on all sides were upset to find out that their own leaders—black and white—had committed crimes during apartheid. The leader of the TRC, Archbishop Desmond Tutu, repeatedly emphasized the need for forgiveness. Not everyone was able to forgive the crimes they experienced or heard about through the TRC, but in bringing out the truth, the hearings took an important step toward bringing the country back together.[6]

Even under apartheid, black and white children sometimes made friends. They did not share the prejudices of their parents.

Challenges in the New South Africa

After the first elections, South Africa's ANC leaders had a great deal to be proud of. They had negotiated a transition from apartheid to democratic rule without a civil war. They won their election by a landslide, promising to lift the people up out of poverty, re-create the damaged education system, and bring services such as electricity and health care to the millions of citizens who had none.

Once they were in power, the ANC faced a whole new set of challenges. None of their leaders had ever governed a country before. They were as dedicated to their people as anyone could be, but they had spent their lives as prisoners, exiles, or street protesters.[7] To make matters worse, South Africa was nearly bankrupt.

Partly because of these challenges, South Africa's new leaders were not able to make as much progress as they hoped. Their country has a wealth of natural resources and a well-developed economy, but the vast majority of people have remained desperately poor. White South Africans, who held all the power and privilege under apartheid, still controlled most of the money, land, and resources. Black, Indian, and coloured people have seen drastic improvements in their lives, but most are still stuck in poverty.

When apartheid ended, the government lifted restrictions on where people could live. Looking for new opportunities, millions of black South Africans moved from the homelands to the cities. Some of them joined friends and family members in the townships. Others, finding nowhere else to live, erected huge shantytowns on the outskirts of the cities.

Life in the shantytowns is hard on everyone. In 1999, five years after the first election, researchers asked children from one shantytown what they wished for. Their requests were simple: less crime, regular trash pickup, public toilets, and easy access to clean water.[8] Some complained that they had no space or light for doing homework because the small shacks in which they lived had no electricity.[9]

By 2009, about one out of every four South Africans was unemployed.[10] In spite of aggressive affirmative action laws, black adults who got little or no education under apartheid were having the hardest time finding work. City streets were filled with people begging for money or selling handmade crafts.

The violence of the final years of apartheid has never completely abated. In 2009, most of South Africa's violence centered on money rather than politics.

Nearly every day, the news was reporting muggings, burglaries, and carjackings. Police were working hard to reduce the crime rate, but many of the country's wealthiest and most educated people were moving to other countries, where they could live in greater safety.

As apartheid was ending, HIV and AIDS were spreading quickly through the population. The HIV virus had infected millions of people, especially in the shantytowns and townships. This disease again broke apart many of the families that had been split up during apartheid. Millions of children lost their parents to the epidemic. Public programs were put in place to help those who became infected, but by 2009, as many as 1,000 South Africans were dying from AIDS-related causes every day.[11]

Hope for the Future

When Nelson Mandela retired at the end of his five-year term as president, South Africans worried that the country might not remain stable.[12] It did. Elections went off smoothly in 1999, 2004, and 2009, and the ANC won easily all three times.

Although they have not accomplished all they hoped, South Africa's current leaders have taken important steps in the right direction. In the first decade after apartheid ended, they brought clean water to 9 million people, electricity to 2 million, and phones to 1.5 million. They integrated the public schools and gave free health care to millions of children.[13]

Improvements like these are essential for a free South Africa. They give people a chance to lead healthier, safer lives, and to work toward better opportunities. Every day, more people have the chance to go to the doctor if they are sick, to call the police if their house is robbed, or to switch on electric lights to work and study in the evenings.

Has the new government done a good enough job? Every five years, South Africans will go back to the polls and decide. Perhaps they will put the ANC in power for many more years, or perhaps they will give control to another party for a while. Either way, every voter's say in that decision will be exactly equal. Every South African—regardless of race, social class, or skin color—gets exactly one vote. Each of them will help decide how progress in their country should continue.

FYInfo
FOR YOUR INFORMATION

In 1995, Taddy Blecher was ready to give up on South Africa. Like many other white, educated citizens of his country, he felt he would have better opportunities overseas. He packed his belongings and even bought a plane ticket, but two weeks before he was supposed to leave, he suddenly doubted himself. After a sleepless night agonizing over his choices, he decided he could not leave his country behind. Instead, he resolved to do something meaningful to help change South Africa for the better.

Blecher founded the world's first free university, CIDA City Campus. He convinced South African corporations to donate buildings, computers, and teachers. He even found a company that would provide lunch for his students. By 1999, he was offering some of South Africa's poorest students a chance to earn a college degree in business at no cost to themselves.

Most of Blecher's students would have had little chance of entering the business world without the education they received at CIDA City Campus. More than half of the students' parents never got beyond primary school. Few had ever touched a computer or held a bank account. Virtually none could afford the cost of other universities. But after finishing a degree at CIDA City Campus, they could land jobs with South Africa's best corporations.

Robert Redford (left) and Sir Ben Kingsley present Taddy Blecher (center) with the Skoll Award for Social Entrepreneurship. The award honors those with the most innovative and effective approaches to resolving critical social issues worldwide.

As part of their studies, students at CIDA City Campus must do service projects in their home communities. Students have taught high school, shown taxi drivers how to get insurance, and helped street vendors manage their finances. The university draws students from all over the country, so its students help people all over South Africa every day.[14]

Chronology

1976	On June 16, police massacre protesting schoolchildren in Soweto, and massive riots follow.
1977	Black Consciousness leader Steve Biko is killed in prison.
1980s	Countries around the world place trade restrictions on South Africa.
1984–1986	Mass uprisings throw the black townships into chaos.
1989	South Africa's presidents hold secret peace talks with Nelson Mandela.
1990	
February 2	F.W. de Klerk announces that he will take the first major steps to end apartheid.
February 11	Mandela is released from prison.
May 2	The government and ANC meet to hold "talks about talks," which pave the way for future negotiations.
August	The ANC agrees to stop its armed struggle.
1991	
June 30	De Klerk's government repeals most apartheid-era laws.
December 20–21	South Africa's political parties come together to negotiate a new constitution.
1992	
March 17	An all-white vote shows overwhelming support for the shift away from apartheid.
June 17	Thirty-eight ANC supporters die in a terrorist massacre.
July 15	Mandela accuses de Klerk of supporting attacks against the ANC, and talks break down.
September	Mandela and de Klerk sign a Record of Understanding.
1993	
March	Negotiations resume.
November 18	Leaders agree on an interim constitution and set a date for democratic elections.
December	Mandela and de Klerk receive the Nobel Peace Prize.
1994	
April 27–28	The ANC wins South Africa's first democratic elections.
May 10	Mandela takes office as the first president of the new South Africa.
1996	
April 16	The Truth and Reconciliation Commission begins hearings.
May 8	South Africa adopts a permanent constitution.
December 10	President Mandela signs the new constitution into law.
1999	
June 2	Democratic elections take place on schedule and keep the ANC in power.
June 14	Thabo Mbeki of the ANC takes office as president.
2004	Mbeki of the ANC is reelected president of South Africa.
2008	Mbeki is pressured to step down, and Jacob Zuma assumes power.
2009	Zuma is elected president of South Africa, keeping the ANC in power.

Timeline in History

1913	The South African government restricts black land ownership. The ANC is founded.
1918	Nelson Mandela is born.
1920	South African leaders create laws that restrict job opportunities for blacks.
1948	Apartheid begins. Alan Paton publishes *Cry, the Beloved Country*.
1952	Resistance groups organize the nonviolent Defiance Campaign.
1954	In the United States, segregation is outlawed in schools.
1955	The Montgomery bus boycott begins in the United States. Antiapartheid groups adopt the Freedom Charter at the Congress of the People.
1956	Members of the Congress of the People are arrested for treason.
1959	The Pan-Africanist Congress (PAC) breaks away from the African National Congress (ANC).
1960	South African police massacre peaceful protesters at Sharpeville. Apartheid leaders ban the ANC and the PAC.
1961	The Berlin Wall is built in Germany. The Treason Trial ends, and all participants are found not guilty. Nelson Mandela founds Umkhonto we Sizwe ("the Spear of Africa").
1963	Apartheid government begins holding prisoners for up to 90 days without trial. In the United States, Martin Luther King Jr. delivers his "I Have a Dream" speech.
1964	Leaders of Umkhonto we Sizwe, including Mandela, are sentenced to life in prison.
1968	Martin Luther King Jr. is assassinated.
1969	Steve Biko founds the Black Consciousness movement.
1976	Police massacre protesting schoolchildren in Soweto.
1977	Biko is killed in prison.
1980s	Growing violence threatens apartheid's rule in South Africa.
1980	South Africa's neighbor Zimbabwe gains independence.
1989	The Berlin Wall falls in Germany.
1990	South African President F.W. de Klerk begins to dismantle apartheid. South Africa's neighbor Namibia gains independence. It is one of the last African countries to do so.
1991	The Soviet Union falls. South African writer Nadine Gordimer wins the Nobel Prize for literature.
1992	Race riots erupt in Los Angeles, United States.
1994	The ANC wins South Africa's first democratic election. Nelson Mandela becomes the country's first democratically elected president. Racial violence descends on Rwanda as Hutus massacre Tutsis.
1996	South Africa adopts a permanent constitution.
2003	South African writer J.M. Coetzee wins the Nobel Prize for literature.
2008	Barack Obama is elected the first black president of the United States.
2009	July 18, Nelson Mandela's birthday, is declared Mandela Day.
2010	South Africa hosts the soccer World Cup.

Chapter Notes

Chapter 1. No Easy Journey

1. Nelson Mandela, *Long Walk to Freedom* (Boston: Little, Brown, and Company, 1995), p. 563.
2. Ibid., pp. 563–564.
3. Shaun Johnson, "The Day Mandela Came Home," *Cape Town Calling: From Mandela to Theroux in the Mother City*, edited by Justin Fox (Cape Town: Tafelberg, 2007), pp. 39-40.
4. Mandela, p. 564.
5. Johnson, p. 40.
6. Mandela, p. 565.
7. Ibid., pp. 565–566.
8. Rita M. Byrnes, ed., "History," *South Africa: A Country Study* (Washington: GPO for the Library of Congress, 1996), http://countrystudies.us/South-africa/

Chapter 2. Building Apartheid

1. South African History Online, "The 1948 Election and the National Party Victory," http://www.sahistory.org.za/pages/governance-projects/SA-1948-1976/1948-election.htm
2. Nelson Mandela, *Long Walk to Freedom*, (Boston: Little, Brown, and Company, 1995), pp. 110–112.
3. South African History Online.
4. Mike Nicol, *The Waiting Country: A South African Witness* (London: Victor Gollanz, 1995), p. 53.
5. Miriam and Mark Mathabane, *Miriam's Song* (New York: Simon and Schuster, 2000), pp. 43–44.
6. Carol Lazar, *Women of South Africa: Their Fight for Freedom* (Boston: Little, Brown, and Company, 1993), pp. 8–10.
7. Qtd. in Mandela, p. 167.
8. Mathabane, pp. 16–18.
9. Allister Sparks, *Beyond the Miracle: Inside the New South Africa* (Johannesburg: Jonathan Ball Publishers, 2003), pp. 69–70.
10. South African History Online, "Helen Joseph," http://www.sahistory.org.za/pages/people/bios/joseph,h.htm
11. South African History Online, "The Nobel Prize in Literature," http://www.sahistory.org.za/pages/people/nobel%20prize/nobel-prize-literature.htm
12. Sparks, pp. 73-74.

Chapter 3. The Fight for Freedom

1. Nelson Mandela, *Long Walk to Freedom* (Boston: Little, Brown, and Company, 1995), pp. 128–132.
2. Ibid., p. 144.
3. Ibid., p. 174.
4. Ibid, p. 172–175.
5. South African History Online, "The Freedom Charter: Significance of the Congress of the People and the Freedom Charter," http://www.sahistory.org.za/pages/governance-projects/freedom-charter/07_charter_significance.htm
6. Mandela, p. 259.
7. South African History Online, "The Sharpeville Massacre, 1960," http://www.sahistory.org.za/pages/governance-projects/sharpeville/menu.htm
8. Mandela, pp. 238.
9. South African History Online, "The Event: Eyewitness Accounts," "The Sharpeville Massacre, 1960."
10. Ibid.
11. Rita M. Byrnes, ed., "Black Resistance in the 1950s," *South Africa: A Country Study* (Washington: GPO for the Library of Congress, 1996), http://countrystudies.us/south-africa/26.htm
12. Mandela, p. 239.
13. Ibid., p. 243.
14. Ibid., p. 285.
15. Byrnes, ed., "The ANC and the PAC Turn to Violence," *South Africa: A Country Study* (Washington: GPO for the Library of Congress, 1996), http://countrystudies.us/south-africa/27.htm
16. South African History Online, "Umkhonto we Sizwe—The Formation of the MK," http://www.sahistory.org.za/pages/governance-projects/organisations/MK/MKframeset.htm
17. Mandela, pp. 277–279.
18. South African History Online, "The Rivonia Trial and Lillieslief Farm," http://www.sahistory.org.za/pages/governance-projects/rivonia-liliesleaf/rivonia-trial.htm
19. Mandela, p. 351.
20. Ibid., p. 353.
21. Ibid., p. 368.
22. Ibid., p. 376.

Chapter Notes

23. Ibid, pp. 227–229.
24. South African History Online, "The Black Consciousness Movement in South Africa's Freedom Struggle," http://www.sahistory.org.za/pages/governance-projects/black-consciousness/biko/biko-frameset.htm and "Defining Black Consciousness," http://www.sahistory.org.za/pages/governance-projects/black-consciousness/biko/history.htm#defn
25. South African History Online, "Inkatha Freedom Party," http://www.sahistory.org.za/pages/governance-projects/organisations/ifp/ifp.htm and "Mangosuthu Gatsha Buthelezi," http://www.sahistory.org.za/pages/people/bios/buthelezi-mg.htm

Chapter 4. Apartheid Falls Apart

1. South African History Online, "The Youth Struggle, The 1976 Students' Revolts: Day One—June 16," http://www.sahistory.org.za/pages/governance-projects/june16/day1.htm
2. Ibid., "Background," http://www.sahistory.org.za/pages/governance-projects/june16/june16.htm
3. Miriam and Mark Mathabane, *Miriam's Song* (New York: Simon and Schuster, 2000), pp. 18–19.
4. South African History Online, "Background."
5. South African History Online, "Day One—June 16."
6. Ibid.
7. Mathabane, pp. 67–69.
8. South African History Online, "Day One—June 16."
9. Mathabane, pp. 67–69.
10. Rita M. Byrnes, ed., "The Contradictions of Apartheid," *South Africa: A Country Study* (Washington: GPO for the Library of Congress, 1996), http://countrystudies.us/south-africa/31.htm
11. Allister Sparks, *Beyond the Miracle: Inside the New South Africa* (Johannesburg: Jonathan Ball Publishers, 2003), p. 22.
12. Ibid., p. 148.
13. Ibid., pp. 151–152.
14. Mathabane, pp. 181–203.
15. Byrnes, ed., "Limited Reforms," http://countrystudies.us/south-africa/33.htm

16. Ibid., "Divisions in the White Community," http://countrystudies.us/south-africa/32.htm
17. Ibid., "Limited Reforms."
18. Nelson Mandela, *Long Walk to Freedom* (Boston: Little, Brown, and Company, 1995), p. 556.
19. Byrnes, ed., "Dismantling Apartheid, 1990–94," http://countrystudies.us/south-africa/34.htm
20. Mandela, p. 611.
21. Ibid., p. 411.
22. Ibid., pp. 467–468.
23. Ibid., pp. 419–420.

Chapter 5. Democracy

1. Mike Nicol, *The Waiting Country: A South African Witness* (London: Victor Gollancz, 1995), pp. 23–24.
2. Ibid., p. 28.
3. Ibid., pp. 23–24.
4. Paul Bell, Pat Schwartz, and Paul Weinberg, *An End to Waiting* (Johannesburg: Independent Electoral Commission, 1995), p. 31.
5. Ibid., p. 79.
6. South African History Online, "Truth and Reconciliation Commission," http://www.sahistory.org.za/pages/governance-projects/TRC/index.htm
7. Allister Sparks, *Beyond the Miracle: Inside the New South Africa* (Johannesburg: Jonathan Ball Publishers, 2003), p. 29.
8. Jill Swart-Kruger, ed., *Growing Up in Canaansland: Children's Recommendations on Improving the Squatter Camp Environment* (Pretoria: Human Sciences Research Council, 1999), p. 32.
9. Ibid., p. 45.
10. Central Intelligence Agency: The World Factbook, "South Africa," https://www.cia.gov/library/publications/the-world-factbook/geos/sf.html
11. South African History Online, "HIV/AIDS Timeline," http://www.sahistory.org.za/pages/chronology/special-chrono/society/hiv-aids.html
12. Sparks, p. 251.
13. Ibid., p. 3.
14. Ibid., pp. 235–238.

Further Reading

For Young Readers

Blauer, Ettigale, and Jason Lauré. *South Africa*. New York: Children's Press, 2006.

The Diagram Group. *History of Southern Africa*. New York: Facts on File, Inc., 2003.

Downing, David. *Witness to History: Apartheid in South Africa*. Chicago: Heinemann Library, 2004.

Mathabane, Miriam and Mark. *Miriam's Song*. New York: Simon and Schuster, 2000.

Maxim, Lionel J. *Madiba the Rainbow Man*. Wynberg, South Africa: Asjen CC, 1997.

Sheehan, Sean. *South Africa Since Apartheid*. Great Britain: Hodder Wayland, 2002.

Tames, Richard. *End of Apartheid: A New South Africa*. Chicago: Heinemann Library, 2001.

Fiction For Young Readers

Naidoo, Beverly. *Journey to Jo'burg: A South African Story*. New York: HarperTrophy, 1998.

————. *No Turning Back: A Novel of South Africa*. New York: HarperCollins Publishers, 1997.

Paton, Alan. *Cry, the Beloved Country*. New York: Scribner, 2003.

Works Consulted

Bell, Paul, Pat Schwartz, and Paul Weinberg. *An End to Waiting*. Johannesburg: Independent Electoral Commission, 1995.

Byrnes, Rita M., ed. *South Africa: A Country Study*. Washington: GPO for the Library of Congress, 1996. http://countrystudies.us/south-africa/

CIA: The World Factbook. "South Africa" (updated November 20, 2008). https://www.cia.gov/library/publications/the-world-factbook/geos/sf.html

Johnson, Shaun. "The Day Mandela Came Home." *Cape Town Calling: From Mandela to Theroux in the Mother City*. Justin Fox, ed. Cape Town: Tafelberg, 2007.

Lazar, Carol. *Women of South Africa: Their Fight for Freedom*. Boston: Little, Brown, and Company, 1993.

Mandela, Nelson. *Long Walk to Freedom*. Boston: Little, Brown, and Company, 1995.

Mathabane, Miriam and Mark. *Miriam's Song*. New York: Simon and Schuster, 2000.

Nicol, Mike. *The Waiting Country: A South African Witness*. London: Victor Gollancz, 1995.

South African History Online. http://www.sahistory.org.za/pages/index/menu.htm

Sparks, Allister. *Beyond the Miracle: Inside the New South Africa*. Cape Town: Jonathan Ball Publishers, 2003.

Swart-Kruger, Jill, ed. *Growing Up in Canaansland: Children's Recommendations on Improving the Squatter Camp Environment*. Pretoria: Human Sciences Research Council, 1999.

On the Internet

South Africa History Online: *History Classroom*
http://www.sahistory.org.za/classroom/index.htm

South Africa Info: *South Africa's National Anthem*
http://www.southafrica.info/about/history/anthem.htm

YouTube: *CIDA City Campus, South Africa*
http://www.youtube.com/watch?v=Cgwf1HniVT4

Glossary

affirmative action—A policy that improves access to jobs and education for people who have suffered discrimination.

African National Congress (ANC)—*During apartheid:* A major antiapartheid resistance group. ANC members long held that racial reconciliation, not black dominance, was best for South Africa. *Today:* One of South Africa's political parties.

Afrikaans (af-ree-KAHNZ)—One of the eleven official languages of South Africa. Afrikaans is very similar to Dutch; it descended from the Dutch language spoken by early white settlers in southern Africa.

Afrikaner (af-ree-KAHN-er)—An Afrikaans-speaking South African of Dutch or mixed-European descent.

Amandla! . . . Ngawethu! (ah-MAAHN-dlah . . . ah-WAAY-too)—A call-and-response chant used by the resistance during apartheid. In Zulu and Xhosa, two of South Africa's official languages, it means "Power . . . belongs to the people!"

apartheid (uh-PART-hide)—A set of strict laws that were designed to keep all South Africans separated by race, with white people holding power over all other groups.

ban—To place under a banning order.

banning order—An order by the apartheid government that made it illegal for a person to travel freely, attend meetings, or engage in political activities.

Bantu (BAN-too) **Education**—The education system for black South Africans during apartheid.

coloured (KUH-lurd)—Of mixed race.

homeland—A small, overcrowded tract of land where a specific group of black South Africans, such as the Zulu or Xhosa, was supposed to live.

Independent Electoral Commission—A permanent body created by the constitution to ensure safe and fair elections in South Africa.

Inkatha (in-KAH-thuh) **Freedom Party (IFP)**—*During apartheid:* A Zulu-dominated political group that cooperated with apartheid leaders and right-wing Afrikaners. *Today:* One of South Africa's political parties.

martial (MAR-shul) **law**—A state of law imposed by military force rather than by ordinary police.

National Party—The political party that ruled South Africa during apartheid.

Pan Africanist Congress (PAC)—*During apartheid:* A major antiapartheid resistance group whose members generally believed that black people should determine the future of South Africa without the influence of whites. *Today:* One of South Africa's political parties.

pass—An identification document that black people were forced to carry during apartheid.

rand—The currency of South Africa.

sabotage (SAB-uh-tahj)—An attack meant to undermine a cause.

shantytown (SHAN-tee-town)—A settlement of very poor people who live in shacks built from scavenged materials.

supremacy (suh-PREM-uh-see)—Power or authority.

tear (TEER) **gas**—A gas that causes sneezing, coughing, and painful burning and watering of the eyes.

township—*During apartheid:* An urban area where non-white city dwellers were required to live. *Today:* Urban areas where South Africa's poorest citizens live. Although laws no longer require that these areas be segregated by race, almost everyone who lives in the townships is still non-white.

Umkhonto we Sizwe (oom-KOHN-toh-way-SEEZ-way)—"The Spear of Africa": The armed wing of the African National Congress.

Zulu (ZOO-loo)—The language and people of one of South Africa's many black cultures.

Index